Zoom In on

Science Concepts

Gravity

Andrea Rivera

abdopublishing.com

Published by Abdo Zoom™, PO Box 398166, Minneapolis, Minnesota 55439. Copyright © 2018 by Abdo Consulting Group, Inc. International copyrights reserved in all countries. No part of this book may be reproduced in any form without written permission from the publisher. Abdo Zoom™ is a trademark and logo of Abdo Consulting Group, Inc.

Printed in the United States of America, North Mankato, Minnesota
052017
092017

THIS BOOK CONTAINS RECYCLED MATERIALS

Front Cover: Martin Barraud/iStockphoto
Interior Photos: Martin Barraud/iStockphoto, 1; Shutterstock Images, 4–5; NASA/ESA/ J. Dalcanton/B.F. Williams/ L.C. Johnson (University of Washington)/PHAT team/R. Gendler, 6–7; Ames/JPL-Caltech/NASA, 7; Igor Zh/ Shutterstock Images, 8; iStockphoto, 9, 12–13, 14, 15, 17, 18, 19; NASA, 10; Jeff Schmaltz/LANCE/EOSDIS MODIS Rapid Response Team/GSFC/NASA, 11; Judy Schmidt/ESA/Hubble & NASA, 21

Editor: Brienna Rossiter
Series Designer: Madeline Berger
Art Direction: Dorothy Toth

Publisher's Cataloging-in-Publication Data
Names: Rivera, Andrea, author.
Title: Gravity / by Andrea Rivera.
Description: Minneapolis, MN : Abdo Zoom, 2018. | Series: Science concepts |
    Includes bibliographical references and index.
Identifiers: LCCN 2017931238 | ISBN 9781532120510 (lib. bdg.) |
    ISBN 978164797623 (ebook) | ISBN 978164798187 (Read-to-me ebook)
Subjects: LCSH: Gravity--Juvenile literature. | Gravitation--Juvenile literature.
Classification: DDC 531/.14--dc23
LC record available at http://lccn.loc.gov/2017931238

Table of Contents

Science 4

Technology. 8

Engineering 12

Art 16

Math 18

Key Stats. 20

Glossary 22

Booklinks 23

Index 24

Science

Gravity is a **force**. It pulls objects together. On Earth it pulls objects toward the ground. It keeps them from floating off into space.

Gravity is all over the **universe**. Planets, moons, and stars all have gravity. It holds them in place.

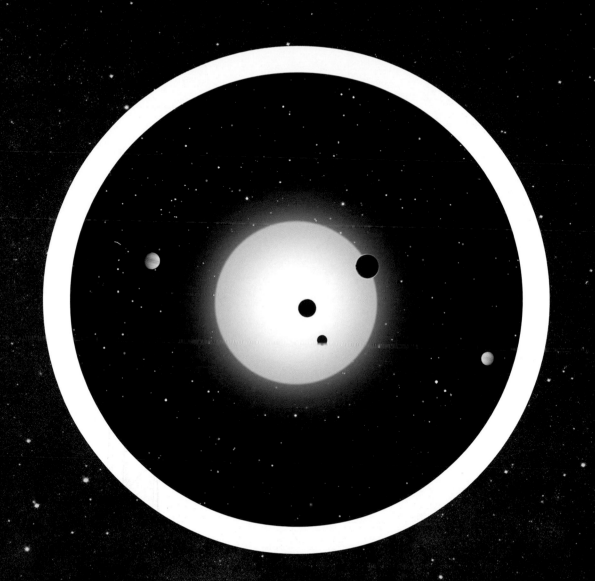

Bigger objects have stronger gravity. They can pull smaller objects toward them.

This can cause the smaller objects to **orbit** larger ones.

Satellites in outer space orbit Earth.

They send back
data or pictures.

Gravity makes falling objects go faster and faster.

Roller coasters go down hills. Gravity makes them speed up.

To go up hills, roller coasters must go against gravity. This slows them down.

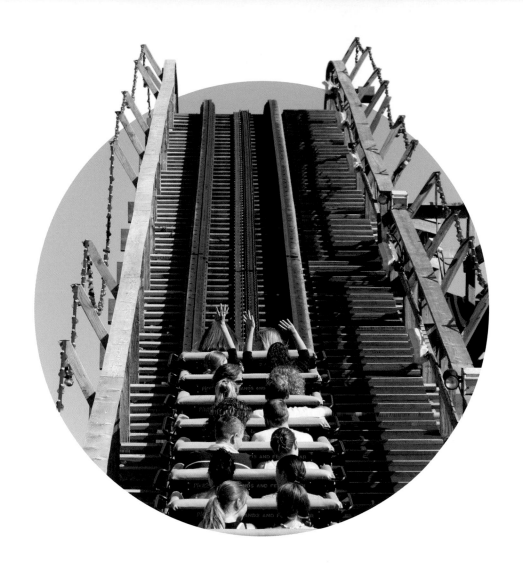

Roller coasters use chains.
The chains pull the cars
up the biggest hills.

Art

Some artists use gravity to paint. They pour paint on a **canvas**. Gravity makes the paint drip down.

Math

The moon is smaller than Earth. So gravity on the moon is weaker. That makes things weigh less there. A dog might weigh 65 pounds (29 kg) on Earth.

But it would weigh about
11 pounds (5 kg) on the moon.

Key Stats

- Gravity works on everything in the universe.

- Without gravity, stars and planets would swirl around and smash into each other.

- Our solar system has eight planets. Each planet has a different amount of gravity.

- Gravity is stronger on Jupiter, the largest planet. Something that weighs 50 pounds (23 kg) on Earth would weigh 118 pounds (54 kg) on Jupiter.

Glossary

canvas - a strong cloth that artists paint on.

data - information that is collected to study or plan something.

force - a push or pull that causes a change in motion.

orbit - to travel around something, usually in an oval path.

satellite - a device or object that travels around a planet.

universe - all of outer space.

Booklinks

For more information on
gravity, please visit
abdobooklinks.com

 In on STEAM!

Learn even more with the Abdo Zoom
STEAM database. Check out
abdozoom.com for more information.

Index

artists, 16

data, 11

dog, 18

Earth, 4, 10, 18

moons, 6, 18, 19

orbit, 9

paint, 16

planets, 6

roller coasters, 13, 14, 15

satellites, 10

space, 4

stars, 6

universe, 6